Haida Songs

By

John Reed Swanton

First published in 1912

Published by Left of Brain Books

Copyright © 2023 Left of Brain Books

ISBN 978-1-397-66976-6

First Edition

All rights reserved. No part of this publication may be reproduced, distributed, or transmitted in any form or by any means, including photocopying, recording, or other electronic or mechanical methods, without the prior written permission of the publisher, except in the case of brief quotations permitted by copyright law. Left of Brain Books is a division of Left Of Brain Onboarding Pty Ltd.

PUBLISHER'S PREFACE

About the Book

"The Haida are a Canadian Native American group which lives on the Queen Charlotte Islands, just off the coast of British Columbia. This is the triangular archipelago which looks like it is a piece broken off of Alaska. This collection of Haida songs, collected early in the 20th century, gives many insights into Haida culture, including class divisions, belief in reincarnation, and the status of women. This etext is presented with the full Haida interlinear text."

(Quote from sacred-texts.com)

About the Author

John Reed Swanton (1873 - 1958)

"John Reed Swanton (19 February 1873 - 2 May 1958) was an American anthropologist who worked with Native American peoples throughout the United States.

Born in Gardiner, Maine, Swanton's work in the fields of ethnology and ethnohistory is well recognized. He is particularly noted for his work with indigenous peoples of the Southeast and Pacific Northwest. He attended Harvard University from which he earned a Masters in 1897 and a doctorate in 1900. His mentor was the famous Franz Boas, whose influence on Swanton is clear. Following his education, he did fieldwork in the Northwest, and then began working for the Bureau of

American Ethnology, where he remained employed for almost 40 years.

In his early career in the Northwest, he mostly worked with the Tlingit and Haida. He produced two extensive compilations of Haida stories and myths, and transcribed many of them in Haida. These transcriptions have served as the basis for Robert Bringhurst's recent (1999) translation of the poetry of Haida mythtellers Skaay and Gandl. Swanton spent roughly a year with the Haida.

After that, Swanton studied Muskogean speaking peoples in Texas, Louisiana, and Oklahoma. He published extensively on the Creek people, Chickasaw, and Choctaw as well as recording information about many other less well-known groups, such as the Biloxi and Ofo. He argued in favor of including the Natchez language with the Muskogean language group. His works included partial dictionaries, studies of linguistic relationships, collections of native stories, and studies of social organization. He also worked with Earnest Gouge, a Creek who recorded a large number of traditional Creek stories at Swanton's request. These materials were never published by Swanton, but have recently been republished."

(Quote from wikipedia.org)

CONTENTS

PUBLISHER'S PREFACE
INTRODUCTION 1
CRADLE-SONGS 4
    CHAPTER 1 5
    CHAPTER 2 6
    CHAPTER 3 7
    CHAPTER 4 8
    CHAPTER 5 9
    CHAPTER 6 10
    CHAPTER 7 11
    CHAPTER 8 12
    CHAPTER 9 13
    CHAPTER 10 14
    CHAPTER 11 15
    CHAPTER 12 16
    CHAPTER 13 17
    CHAPTER 14 18
    CHAPTER 15 20
    CHAPTER 16 21
    CHAPTER 17 22
    CHAPTER 18 23
    CHAPTER 19 24
    CHAPTER 20 25
    CHAPTER 21 26
    CHAPTER 22 27
    CHAPTER 23 28
    CHAPTER 24 29
    CHAPTER 25 30
    CHAPTER 26 31
    CHAPTER 27 32
    CHAPTER 28 33
    CHAPTER 29 34

CHAPTER 30	35
CHAPTER 31	36
CHAPTER 32	37
CHAPTER 33	38
CHAPTER 34	40
CHAPTER 35	42
CHAPTER 36	43
CHAPTER 37	44
CHAPTER 38	46
CHAPTER 39	47
CHAPTER 40	49
CHAPTER 41	50
CHAPTER 42	51
CHAPTER 43	52
CHAPTER 44	53
CHAPTER 45	54
CHAPTER 46	55
CHAPTER 47	56
CHAPTER 48	57
CHAPTER 49	58
CHAPTER 50	59
CHAPTER 51	60
CHAPTER 52	61
CHAPTER 53	62
CHAPTER 54	63
CHAPTER 55	64
CHAPTER 56	65
CHAPTER 57	66
CHAPTER 58	67
CHAPTER 59	68
CHAPTER 60	69
CHAPTER 61	70
CHAPTER 62	71
CHAPTER 63	72
CHAPTER 64	73
CHAPTER 65	74
CHAPTER 66	75
CHAPTER 67	76
CHAPTER 68	77
CHAPTER 69	78

- CHAPTER 70 79
- CHAPTER 71 80
- CHAPTER 72 81
- CHAPTER 73 82
- CHAPTER 74 83
- CHAPTER 75 84
- CHAPTER 76 85
- CHAPTER 77 86
- CHAPTER 78 87
- CHAPTER 79 88
- CHAPTER 80 89
- CHAPTER 81 90
- CHAPTER 82 91
- CHAPTER 83 92
- CHAPTER 84 93
- CHAPTER 85 94
- CHAPTER 86 95
- CHAPTER 87 96
- CHAPTER 88 97

MOURNING SONGS 98

- CHAPTER 89 99
- CHAPTER 90 100
- CHAPTER 91 101
- CHAPTER 92 102
- CHAPTER 93 103
- CHAPTER 94 104
- CHAPTER 95 105
- CHAPTER 96 106
- CHAPTER 97 107
- CHAPTER 98 108
- CHAPTER 99 109
- CHAPTER 100 110

MISCELLANEOUS SONGS 111

- CHAPTER 101 112
- CHAPTER 102 113
- CHAPTER 103 114
- CHAPTER 104 115
- CHAPTER 105 116

CHAPTER 106 117

INTRODUCTION

THE following songs were collected by the writer in connection with his work for the Jesup North Pacific Expedition during the winter of 1900-01. The general characteristics of the songs were described in "Contributions to the Ethnology of the Haida" (Publications of the Jesup North Pacific Expedition, Vol. V, p. 121). As has been stated in a discussion of the songs, the cradle-songs are the Property of the various families. For this reason the songs which form the bulk of the collection here presented are arranged according to the families to which they be long. The names of the families will also be found in the publication before referred to.

The following alphabet is used for rendering Haida songs:--

EXPLANATION OF ALPHABET USED IN RENDERING INDIAN SOUNDS

A,

i e,	î	a	ô	o u
î ê	ä	â	(â),	ô û
			a	o u

A obscure a.

i, e, are probably the same sound, intermediate between the continental values of i and e.

î = i in hill.

a has its continental value.

o, u, are probably the same sound, intermediate between the continental values of o and u.

ä = German ä in Bär.

â = aw, in law, only in foreign words.

a o u indicate that the preceding, consonant is pronounced with a, o, and u position of the mouth respectively.

	Sonans.	Surd.	Fortis.	Spirans.	Nasal.	
Velar	g̱	q	q!	x	---	
Palatal	g	k	k!	x̱	ñ	
Alveolar	d	t	t!	s	n	
Dental	dj	tc	tc!	---	---	
Labial	b	p	---	---	m	
Lateral	Ḻ	L	L!	ɬ	---	l
Laryngeal catch and breathing	?			x		

     h, y, w.

+ indicates great length of preceding vowel.

I have omitted the anterior palatal series, because the Haida sounds which should be classed under that head seem to me accidentally produced, owing to the presence of a following close vowel. p seems to occur only in onomatopoetic elements; b occurs not more than two or three times in strictly Haida words; and m, although considerably more abundant, is by no means common. The catch (?) is used in Masset instead of Skidegate g and , instead of Skidegate x. x is like German ch in Bach; x is similar, but pronounced farther forward. Even among old people the fortis-sounds are frequently reduced to simple pauses. This is particularly true of sounds formed far forward in the mouth. At other times they are uttered with rapidity and force. In recording my texts, I found it difficult to distinguish fortis-sounds from sonants. L sounds something like dl, and L something like tl or kl; in both the tip of the tongue touches the back of the teeth, and the air is expelled at the sides: l is similar, but more of the tongue is laid against the roof of the mouth, and a greater volume of air allowed to escape. ñ is identical with English ng in such words as string.

Words in parentheses in the translations have been added to make the sense of the Indian clearer; bracketed words or parts of words in Indian indicate forms which are inserted in the rhythmic songs, but would be omitted in prose.

CRADLE-SONGS

CHAPTER 1

L'djâ'ada kûdju's Lû Q!ô'na l'nagâ'-i ya'kAlsî'ga L gaya'oga
A woman | it was | when | Skedans | the town of | middle in | its | smoke
sgaqô'nga-lîña's Lû'hao L djâ'adaga-i!
large | may be | when | what (kind of a) woman (are you)!

L'djâ'ada kûdjû'sgu Lga-i gA'nLa-i ge'istA L! sî'qîgAñ[ga]
A woman | was there | Skedans | Creek | out of | they | make the noise
qa-ixuna'ñ-lîña's Lû'hao L djâadâ'ga!
of singing continually | may (not) be | when | what | (kind of a) woman are (you)!

You need not think that the smoke of your house in the middle of Skedans will be as great as when you were a woman (in your previous life upon earth [1]).

You need not think that they will make such a continual noise of singing in Skedans Creek as they used to when you were a woman (in your previous existence).

---

[1] The child is considered a re-incarnation of some dead relative.

CHAPTER 2

Gî'tîns dja'tgañ ya'+nañ sûgwâ+ñ.
Eagle | woman his own | marry | he is saying.
Gî'tîns dja'tgañ ya'+nañ sûgwâ+ñ.
Eagle woman his own marry he is saying.
A'dî'dAxua xA'nhao wa'ga gadjû'+wAn sû'gAñ,
Here behind us | yet | his wife | sits, | he says,
A'dî'dAxua xA'nhao wa'ga gadjû'+wAn sû'gAñ,
Here behind us | yet | his wife | sits, | he says,
HalA' waga daogî'+lgêgo+.
Come | his | let us go up and get.
HalA' waga daogî'+lgêgo+.
Come | his | let us go up and get.
Ha hî'djigana xA'nhao wa'ga gâ'djiwAn sû'wañ,
My | own boy | yet | his (wife) | sits there | he says,
Adî'dExua xA'nhao wa'ga gadjû'+wAn sû'gAñ.
Here behind us | yet | his wife | sits | he says.

He says [1] he is going to marry his own Eagle-Woman,
He says he is going to marry his own Eagle-Woman.
His wife is sitting right behind (the town), he says;
His wife is sitting right behind (the town), he says.
Come, let us go up and get her!
Come, let us go up and get her!
My own boy is saying his wife sits there.
His wife is sitting right behind (the town), he says.

---

[1] "To say" is used here for "to cry."

CHAPTER 3

Ha'lA+ dî'+ga+ skî'nxaLga'go.
Come | for me | all wake up.
Al qâ'+ñgadigwâñga,
I | dreamed about,
Ha ha gasî'n xega'nlîñ. [1]
(Laughing) | they are | going to make a noise about him.

Come, wake up, and listen to me!
I dreamed about it.
Ha, ha! oh, what a noise they are going to make over him (at the potlatch)!

---

[1] Each line of this song is repeated.

CHAPTER 4

Â'+yaña+ â'+yaña+ â'+yaña+ â+yañe a'+yañô,
Be careful, | be careful, | be careful, | be careful, | be careful,
A+îldja'o-gaña a+îldja'o-gaña â'yañê â'yañê.
One who is a noble-man, | one who is a noble-man, | be careful, | be careful.
L gê'ida+lAñ q!a'oxañ [s]gê'+xAn aqâ'dji la' aya+ [1]
Wherever you | sit | into that place | his head | here | you (pl.)
q!aisgêdî'go q!ai'xas gê+ kû'djugwa+ñgasa+ñ.
take off and put away | without anything | he will rove about.
Ayañâ'+a îldja'o-ga'ñañ gan dAñ hî'dja gadjû'gAnê.
Be careful | one who is a noble-man | for | you | sit as a boy belonging to a good family.

Be careful of him, be careful of him, be careful of him, be careful of him, be careful of him.
This nobleman, this nobleman, be careful of him, be careful of him,
Wherever you sit, take off his head and put it away, or he will travel about without anything (i. e., in poverty). [2]
Be careful of this nobleman, etc.

---

[1] Aya is equivalent to wa.
[2] The father of an Eagle girl must give away blankets to this boy's parents, so that he will marry no one else when he grows up. That is what "taking off his head" means. The reference to his poverty is made with mock humility.

CHAPTER 5

Hao gî'na gA+n dAñ îdjagâ'djî'was ê'dji.
This | thing | for | you | sitting as a boy | are.
Hao gî'na gA+n dAñ îdjagâ'djî'was ê'dji.
This | thing | for | you | sitting as a boy | are.
NAñkî'lSLas agA'ñ î'ndaLxagâ'gAnî.
NAñkî'lSLas | himself | made a human being.
Skîls nagâ'ga kûskî'ndias ê'dji, wA'stA Q!aku'ngwi
Property in the house | was, | from it | Rose Spit towards
ga-ilgaga'ñ dA'ñal Ldjûdal.
his flood | with | tidal wave went.
Gwa-isku'n xâ'-idAga-i xA'nhao dAñ nâ'ga lkiä'sigei
North Island | people | even | your | house | towards the door
gut gunL!gA'ndias ê'djî.
are as many as when waves meet each other and are packed close together.
Hao gî'na gA+n dAñ îdjagâ'djî'was ê'dji.
This | thing | for | you | sitting as a boy | are.

This is why you are a boy
This is why you are a boy
NAñkî'lSLas has become a human being.
From the property in his house a flood went towards Rose Spit.
Even from North Island the people are crowded into your house, as when waves meet and are packed together.
That is why you are a boy. [1]

---

[1] The child is born to give these great potlatches. His property is likened to the flood raised in the time of NAñkî'lSLas, and it is said that people will crowd into his house even from North Island.

CHAPTER 6

A+ya+ña'+ ayâ'ñê â'+yañô.
Be careful, | be careful, | be careful.
La hao îldja'oga+n.
He | is a nobleman.

I'+lgiañ wAga'ñ(añ) kû'+skî+twas sê+ Lû tcî'nañ qôniga'-i
(Face) changed | like it | will be wherever your place is | his grand-father | powerful
gî a la qealdî+ga.
for | he looks expectantly.
Ayâ'ñô a o îldja'oga+n.
Be careful, this is a nobleman.

Be careful (of the child), be careful, be careful.
This is going to be a great man.
His face will be changed wherever he may be, when he looks for the coming of his powerful grandfather [1] (and sees him).
Be careful, this is going to be a great man.

---

[1] Skedans and his people called Djê'basa, the Tsimshian chief at Kitkatla, "grand father," and vice versa. After he has become a man, the child's face will look joyous when he sees his Tsimshian friends approach.

CHAPTER 7

A+yañê'+ a'da gua ê'dji tcî'na-i.
Be careful | you | ? | is | grandfather.
A+yañê'+ a'da gua ê'dji NAñkî'lSLas.
Be careful | you | ? | is | grandfather.
A+yañê'+ a'qwês nAñ kîtnâ'ñugîn. [1]
Be careful | this sky | one | touched.

Be careful. Is this you, grandfather? [2]
Be careful. Is this you, NAñkî'lSLas? [3]
Take care. This is perhaps the one that touched the sky. [4]

---

[1] Equivalent to ugA'ñgîn.
[2] The mother refers to ancestors, one of whom is possibly being reborn in her child. "The one that touched the sky" is Many-Ledges (T!ês qoa'naiya), a cliff back of Skedans inhabited by a supernatural being.
[3] The mother refers to ancestors, one of whom is possibly being reborn in her child. "The one that touched the sky" is Many-Ledges (T!ês qoa'naiya), a cliff back of Skedans inhabited by a supernatural being.
[4] The mother refers to ancestors, one of whom is possibly being reborn in her child. "The one that touched the sky" is Many-Ledges (T!ês qoa'naiya), a cliff back of Skedans inhabited by a supernatural being.

CHAPTER 8

U'yatê u'yatê, da'lAñ yA'ta+gadA'ldia'asañ.
Only | only | you | are going to be a yA'ta. [1]
U'yatê u'yatê, da'lAñ yA'ta+gadA'ldia'asañ.
Only | only | you | are going to be a yA'ta.

A tcî'na-i+ lânâ'+ga a'+ñga la xî'-tskûtsga.
His | grandfather's | town | his | he will fill with property seaward.
Dî qê'ndAldigoasî' Lû qî'ñgets nâ'ga-i [a] gut gAn aq!ê'da
You | are of the great people | since | chief's | house | each (near) other | carving qînskitsgâ'dias.
large toward the east (or seaward).
DalA'ñ yA'ta gadA'ldiasañ.
You | a yA'ta | are going to be.

Only you are going to be a yA'ta.
Only you are going to be a yA'ta.
You will fill up your grandfather's town seaward with property.
Since you are of the great people, your chief's houses will have large carvings seaward.
You are going to be a yA'ta.

---

[1] One of high family, who wants for nothing.

CHAPTER 9

WAgaña'ñ gê'il+dia+ñ,
Like it | it has become,
WAgaña'ñ gê'il+dia+ñ,
Like it | it has become,
Gadô'+ GalgA'lda-kun gadô' daLgî'sLdiañ.
Around | GalgA'lda point | around | lots of canoes are coming.
WAgaña'ñ gê'il+dia+ñ,
Like it | it has become,
WAgaña'ñ gê'il+dia+ñ,
Like it | it has become.

Now it has come to pass,
Now it has come to pass.
Plenty of canoes are coming around Point GalgA'lda [1] (to potlatches).
Now it has come to pass,
Now it has come to pass.

---

[1] A point of land southwest of Skedans village.

CHAPTER 10

Gînâ'+ lîñxA'n, gînâ'+ lîñxA'n,
Things | all sorts of, | things | all sorts of,
A L nao da'o-gadAldia'ñ, a L nao da'o-gadA'ldia'ñ.
As many as | grow up well, | as many as | grow up well.
Sqa'gî tî'ga q!alA'lî'nsgua,
Dog-salmon | kill | he is not going to be able,
A L nao da'o-gadA'ldia'ñ, a L nao da'o-gadA'ldia'ñ.
As many as | grow up well, | as many as | grow up well.
A xâ'gu tî'ga q!alAlî'nsgua a,
Halibut | kill | he is not going to be able,
A L nao da'o-gadAldia'ñ, a L nao da'o-gadA'ldia'ñ.
As many as | grow up well, | as many as | grow up well.
Ga'-igîts tî'ga q!alAlî'nsgua,
Cedar-bark | kill (i. e., to chop) | he is not going to be able,
A L nao da'o-gadA'ldia'ñ, a L nao da'o-gadA'ldia'ñ.
As many as | grow up well, | as many as | grow up well.

As many things as grow (he may not kill).
As many things as grow (he may not kill).
Dog salmon he may not kill. [1]
As many as grow, as many as grow.
Halibut he may not kill. [2]
As many as grow, as many as grow.
Cedar-bark he may not kill [3] (i. e., chop),
As many as grow, as many as grow.

---

[1] Because the slaves will do it for him.
[2] Because the slaves will do it for him.
[3] Because the slaves will do it for him.

CHAPTER 11

Gûs lîñ kûdjû'diañ, gûs lîñ kûdjû'diañ?
What | are you for, | what | are you for?
Sgâ'na lî'ñga-i kûdjû'diañ.
Supernatural power | you are going to have | (you) are there for
Gûs lîñ kûdjû'diañ, gûs lîñ kûdjû'diañ?
What | are you for, | what | are you for?

Gatxala'ñ Lu î'sdala-i kî'lskûna
In front of him | canoe to (have) pass | he will not like
Â'hao lîñ kûdjû'diañ
For that | he is going to be
Gûs lîñ kûdjû'diañ, gûs lîñ kûdjû'diañ?
What | are you for, | what | are you for?
Sgâ'na lî'ñga-i kûdjû'diañ.
Supernatural power | you are going to have | (you) are there for.

What are you for, what are you for?
You are to have a supernatural helper.
What are you for, what are you for?
You will not let canoes pass in front of you. [1]
That is what you are for.
What are you for, what are you for?
You are to have a supernatural helper.

---

[1] If people of low family passed close in front of chiefs' houses in their canoes, they might be injured or enslaved.

CHAPTER 12

K!ûstî'ñ gwalî'ñasi, k!ûstî'ñ gwalî'ñasi, wâ'ga qâ'dji la
Two if there were, two if there were, their heads I
dagaga'olîñasi.
would keep.
K!ûstî'ñ gwalî'ñasi, k!ûstî'ñ gwalî'ñasi, wâ'ga qâ'dji la
Two if there were, two if there were, their heads I
dagaga'olîñasi.
would keep.

If there were two (boys), if there were two, I would keep their heads.
If there were two (boys), if there were two, I would keep their heads. [1]

---

[1] As a mother received property from the parents of the girl her son married, she would have received more if she had had two sons. Mothers who did not make these gifts were laughed at.

CHAPTER 13

GA'nhao dAñ djâ'ada-gadjû'gAñ, dAñ djâ'das, dAñ djâ'das,
For | you | are a woman, you | are a woman, | you | are a woman,
dAñ djâ'das, dAñ djâ'das.
you | are a woman, you | are a woman.
GA'nhao dAñ djâ'ada-gadjû'gAñ, dAñ djâ'das, dAñ djâ'das,
For | you | are a woman, you | are a woman, | you | are a woman,
dAñ djâ'das, dAñ djâ'das.
you | are a woman, you | are a woman.
Xâ'na qâ'li lk!iä'na-i kîldâ'lL!xaigaiAgAn dAñ djâ'das, dAñ
Skidegate | Inlet | the woods (i.e. timber) | you are going to command | you | are a woman, | you
djâ'das.
are a woman.

For this you are a woman, you are a woman, you are a woman, you are a woman, you are a woman.
For this you are a woman, you are a woman, you are a woman, you are a woman, you are a woman,
To command the sticks (i.e., house-poles) of Skidegate Inlet, [1] you are a woman, you are a woman.

---

[1] The girls of this family often married Skidegate chiefs. So the girl will command when house-poles are to be raised.

CHAPTER 14

Hao dalA'ñ sgA'nxAnhao ya'tê gadA'ldiganê q!o'ldjat, hao
You | only ones | were brought up well | chief women,
dalA'ñ sgA'nxAnhao ya'tê gadA'ldiganê q!o'ldjat,
You | only ones | were brought up well | chief women,
Q!ô'na-kun gadô' ga Lnda'IL!xaga-iyu.
Skedans point | around | sit in his canoe and come with him.
Hao dalA'ñ sgA'nxAnhao, etc. (four times).
You | only ones , etc.
Tcî'nañ qô'naiya-i gwai'ga+gut al dalA'ñ dAñq!â'-isgidan sû.
Your grand-father | powerful | his islands together | you | pulled | it is said.
A'ñga gî A'ñgaxawâ'yu.
Theirs | to | how they let with it.

Hao dalA'ñ sgA'nxAnhao, etc. (four times)
You | only ones, | etc.
Q!êdAs k!ia'oga gi gaxa-ûxansLiya'-i yu. [1]
Tattoo | for | sit down (or take the position).

You, chief women, are the only ones brought up well enough;
you, chief women, are the only ones brought up well enough,
To sit in (the chief's) canoe and come around Skedans point with him.
You, chief women, are the only ones, etc. (four times),
To pull your powerful grandfather's islands [2] together, they say.

---

[1] Yu is equivalent to hao.

[2] "Your grandfather" is Raven, and the islands are the Haida country and the mainland. Reference is perhaps made to mainland marriages.

You, chief women, are the only ones, etc. (four times),
To sit down to receive tattoo-marks.

CHAPTER 15

Hao a'+gadal, hao a'+gadal, a tcî'na nâ'ga qâ'li+ gut
That | is right, | that | is right, | grandfather's | house | inside | around the
dao [1] gutîlA q!a-iguxanskiä'nsi.
in different parts | sit around in groups (the slaves).
WA lkia'gua gaga'-i nAñ q!a'ouwas la hao agA'ñ gâ'djida
Near the door | far off | one | sits | him | let take care of you
hao ag'Añ gada'lda
let him take care of you
Hao a'+gadal (eight times).
That is right.

That is right, that is right, (the slaves) sit in groups around the inside of your grandfather's house.
Let the one sitting far off near the door take care of you, take care of you.
That is right, that is right, that is right, that is right, that is right, that is right, that is right.

---

[1] Equivalent to ga-i.

CHAPTER 16

Dî L!naxAn gê'ildañ hao a gûdâ'ñgani[hê].
I | like that | became | they used to wish.
WAgaña'ñ ô la gêilsgia'ñ hao ô.
Like that | she became | soon.
Â'haô dalA'ñ sgA'nxAn kî'lsLa-i [1] ya'ta dî gadAldjî'gañ
You | only | chief | only (or fit) | you | are (said of a high family)
hao ô+.

They used to wish that I should be like that.
Like it she soon became.
You are the only ones fit to be chiefs' daughters.

---

[1] Or gî'tsîs ("chief's daughter").

CHAPTER 17

Hao dalA'ñ sgA'nxAn kîlsLa'is [1] ya'ta gadA'ldîgAnkwê;
You | only | chief | are of a high family
Hao dalA'ñ sgA'nxAn kîlsLa'is ya'ta gadA'ldîgAnkwê;
You | only | chief | are of a high family
Gî L! (aya+) q!otgâ'ñdixan djâ'gadA'ñganî.
For they | used to be soliciting | (they) tried to get the woman a long time.
Hao dalA'ñ sgA'nxAn kîlsLa'is ya'ta gadA'ldîgAnkwê;
You | only | chief | are of a high family
Hao dalA'ñ sgA'nxAn kîlsLa'is ya'ta gadA'ldîgAnkwê;
You | only | chief | are of a high family

You alone are fit to be a chief woman,
You alone are fit to be a chief woman.
For (you) they begged a long time (to obtain you in marriage).
You alone are fit to be a chief woman,
You alone are fit to be a chief woman.

---

[1] The second verse of this song is identical with this one, except that q!o'ldjat ("chief woman") is substituted for kîlsLa'is wherever it occurs.

CHAPTER 18

HalA' ga'gîñ gao-o (eight times)
Come, | let her sit on my lap (or "let us have her")
Ga ga'os waLû'xAn la gu'tgi gagaga'ñgao gu'tgî ska'ndîgo lA.
The villages | all | to each other | hand (her) | to each other hand.
La sgun ga'gîñûgwâ'ñ, la sgun ga'gîñûgwâ'ñ
I | only | take care of her now, | I | only | take care of her now.
HalA' ga'gîñ gao-o (several times).

come, let her sit on my lap.
Come, let her sit on my lap! (eight times)
All the villages used to hand her to one another.
Now only I take care of her, now only I take care of her. [1]
Come, let her sit on my lap! (several times)

---

[1] This means that all the people of all villages used to be slaves of this family, and so took care of the baby, but now the mother has to do it all herself.

CHAPTER 19

Gû'sLao gûdjâ'+gaña [1] dalA'ñ ga kî'ñgatsgas ga dâ daogîl
Why | your daughters | you | to news went down | what did you come after,
gadâ'lañ?
well brought up one?
Ga gîña'ñ a gî xA'nhao L! qâ'yîñgâ'ña gê'da gagîhîña'ñ
Crying for (no one) they attend you place where she is crying
gaga'ogwañ gadAl, gê'da gagîhîña'ñ gaga'ogwañ gadAl.
lying about, | well brought up one, | place where she is crying | lying about, | well brought up one.

On account of what news of your daughters' going down to you (to The Land of Souls) did you come up for something, well brought up ones?
There is now no one to attend to you on account of your crying, where you are crying about (because there are now no slaves), well brought up one, where you are crying about, well brought up one.

---

[1] The second verse of this song is identical with this one, except that ûgô'ñgaña ("your fathers") is said to be substituted for the words gûdjă+gaña ("your daughters"), but gô'ñga is properly applied only to a man's father.

CHAPTER 20

L!a sgA'nxAn L! gêidAñ sû'ga. L!a sgA'nxAn hao gêidAñ
Those | only | are that way, | they | say. Those | only | are that way,
L! sû'ga.
they say.
GAm iL! La geitgâ'ñañ L! sû'ga.
Not | (with) us | however | it was that way | they | say.

They alone belong to a high family, they say. They alone belong to a high family, they say.
But it is not that way with us, they say.

CHAPTER 21 [1]

Ha LA ha La+ ha Lê'+, ha LA ha La+ ha Lê+.
(Laughter)
Â'ga lglga'odîgAn sgoa'na gwê+,
Here is where | black ground used to be | one | [of them],
Ha LA ha La+ ha Lê'+, ha LA ha La+ ha Lê+.
(Laughter)
A gâ'ldjidAs [2] gâ'ñañ. A gâ'ldjidAs gâ'ñañ.
Crow | like a, | crow | like a.

Ha LA ha La+ ha Lê'+, ha LA ha La+ ha Lê+.
Here is where one of the black tattoo-marks used to be, [3]
Ha LA ha La+ ha Lê'+, ha LA ha La+ ha Lê+.
(Black) just like a crow, (black) just like a crow.

---

[1] This song has to be sung last.
[2] The baby word for "crow."
[3] Probably this refers to the place where the child is supposed to have been tattooed in her former existence on earth.

CHAPTER 22

Hao tcî'nAñ lanâ'ga gua dâ dâ'ga.
Your grandfather's | town | ? | you | own.
Ga'godiya-i gua sgâ'naga, Ga'godiya-i gua sgâ'naga.
Lies | large | ? | is it powerful, Lies | large | ? | is it powerful.
Hao tcî'nAñ lanâ'ga gua dâ dâ'ga.
Your grandfather's | town | ? | you | own.
Qî'ngodiya-i gua sgâ'naga, Qî'ngodiya-i gua sgâ'naga.
Lies down greatly | ? | is it powerful, Lies down greatly | ? | is it powerful.
Hao tcî'nAñ xal tc!â'anuga dâ dâ'ga uyâ'te gâ'djuyañ.
Your grand-father's | copper | fire | you | own | you only are fit | to sit | greatly.

Do you own your grandfather's town ?
Lying large, has it supernatural power? Lying large, has it supernatural power'
Do you own your grandfather's town?
Lying greatly, has it supernatural power? Lying greatly, has it supernatural power?
You only are fit, sitting greatly, to own your grandfather's copper-fire.

CHAPTER 23 [1]

Nô'+ gunatô+ na+ gunatô+ (six times)
Wa+ gîtcî [2] q!ayAm gwa'tAksta nalnîgAn ahô'yûda
down river (?) | near | cry (?)
wâlsî'mgîgyêt [3] dAmgî+ [4] q!adô+
noble men
No+ gûnatô'+ na+ gûnatô'+, no+ gûnatô'+ na+ gûnatô'+.

---

[1] This and the following song are unintelligible, although a number of words may be recognized.
[2] Perhaps gîsi ("down river").
[3] The translation of this word applies only to the latter part of the word, excluding the first three letters.
[4] DAm indicates future.

CHAPTER 24

Hê-ê-ê-ê+ gwâ'ldAma aga'-i (six times)
HA'naagê hê-ê-ê-ê+ gwâ'ldAma aga'-i ha-a-dî+ gîtcî q!al
Woman
mâs (a) nî'cîna algû'[1] ha-a-dî+ gîl bêlha algu
not (?)haliotis not (?)
Hê-ê-ê-ê+ gwâ'ldAma aga'-i i (three times).

---

[1] Probably a'lgE ("not"), or lgu ("small").

CHAPTER 25

Dî'nAñ djat î'+ngadju+
My child | a woman | (comes out having) married,
Dî'nAñ djat î'+ngadju+
My child | a woman | (comes out having) married,
[Aq!a] Q!aiya'-i aq!ôlgû'stA+,
Q!aiya'-i | from the top of,
Dî'nAñ djat î'+ngadju+
My child | a woman | (comes out having) married,
Dî'nAñ djat î'+ngadju+.
My child | a woman | (comes out having) married.

My child comes out married,
My child comes out married,
From the top of (Mount) Q!aiya'-i,
My child comes out married,
My child comes out married.

CHAPTER 26

Gît'î'n-djatsgañ yâ'nañ++ sû'++gañ;
Eagle-woman | his own | has already married, | he is saying;
Gît'î'n-djatsgañ yâ'nañ++ sû'++gañ;
Eagle-woman | his own | has already married, | he is saying;
Adî'dAxua xA'nhao wa'ga gâ'djiwañ sû.
Near right behind [the town] | even | his | sits greatly, he says.
Ha'lai wa'ga da'ogîlkûxaogô;
Come, | his (wife) | let its all go up and get
Ha'lai wa'ga da'ogîlkûxaogô;
Come, | his (wife) | let its all go up and get
Adî'dAxua xA'nhao wa'ga gâ'djiwañ sû.
Near right behind the house | even | his | sits greatly, he says.

He is saying he has married an Eagle woman;
He is saying he has married an Eagle woman.
He says she sits greatly right behind (the town).
Come, let us all go up and get her!
Come, let us all go up and get her! [1]
He says she sits greatly right behind (the town).

---

[1] This refers to the marriage customs.

CHAPTER 27

AgA'ñ lê++dî'gô+, AgA'ñ lê++dî'gô+, Lgalai'gûl djîna's.
Get ready (for him), | get ready (for him), | Lgalai'gûl | women of.
Î'sîñ î'dja kûdjû'diañ ê'++ya a î'ldjao î ai+ + î'ldjao.
Again | it is a boy, | here nobleman, | nobleman.

Get ready for him, get ready for him, [1] women of the Lgalai'gûl [2] family.
Again it is a boy. [3]

---

[1] That is, to marry him.
[2] An extinct branch of the Gî'tîns of Skidegate.
[3] Indicating that boys were scarce.

CHAPTER 28 [1]

Glä'Lû Xâ'na qâ'li, giä'lû Xâ'na qâ'li,
At the time | Skidegate | Inlet, | at the time | Skidegate | Inlet,
DA'ñliai dâ L!da'ogo-ulaiya,
To swell up | you | burst (on that day),
Sgalê îstâ'ûli kî'lsLa-i (four times).
Secret Society | having one day [or morning], | chief.
Ga-i lA î'stâ-ûl kî'lsLa-i (four times).
That | do one day (again), | chief.
Ga'odjaos ga'-ila îstâ'ûl kî'lsLa-i.
Drum (town) | at that place | do it some day, | chief.

Skidegate Inlet, Skidegate Inlet.
When you burst with swelling,
You had the Secret Society perform one day, chief.
Do it again, chief!
Do it one day at Drum Town, chief! [2]

---

[1] The oldest of the set.
[2] Once when there was a great famine in Skidegate Inlet, the chief of Drum Town had enough property to hold a potlatch and save every one from starvation.

CHAPTER 29

DalA'ñ sgu'nxAn gua+ â'hao qîndia'haowus
You | only | ? | here | look about
Tcî'nañ Ik!ia'nga A'ñga dalA'n hao ha-iludâ'lL!xa ûya'te
Grandfather's (i.e., Raven peoples')| timbers | yours | you | got all out of woods | the only fit to do
gadA'ldîgwa'ñ.
highly moving around.
Uyatê' gâ'dAldiañ, uyatê' gâ'dAldiañ, kî'lsLa-i ya'ta
Only | fit | highly moving around, | only | fit | highly moving around, | chief | fit to be
gâ'dAldiañ.
highly moving around.

Are you the only ones who sit looking about?
You are the only ones fit to get all your grandfather's timbers [1] out of the woods, chiefs highly moving around.
Highly moving around, highly moving around, chiefs highly moving around.

---

[1] That is, the Raven peoples' house-timbers. The baby is addressed.

CHAPTER 30

NAñkî'lSLas gôñgâ'+ qîndjî'wayû hao hao qînxiê'ndalAñ.
NAñkî'lSLas's | father | a great one, | such a great one coming along.
Gua+ qîngê'dao î+dja'n sû qî'nlgalwañ.
Halloo! | great chief | is | he says | great one moving about.
Gua'+ qwîga (gî) gî'na gagîtlûgîn û'hao hao îs
halloo! | sky to | something | stretched up (like a rope) | he is there, | it is he
qînxiê'ndAl-Añgua'.
great one moving along.
Qîñgê'do î+dja'n sû qî'ñlgAlwAñ gua'.
Great chief | is | he says | great moving about, | halloo!

He says it is NAñkî'lSLas's great father moving along so greatly.
Halloo, great chief moving about!
Halloo! he moves along greatly like something extending to the sky.
Halloo great chief moving about! [1]

---

[1]NAñkî'lSLas's father would be an Eagle, and the mother pretends that he is reborn in her child.

CHAPTER 31

Â'gua kîlsLa'-i agA'ñ inâ'sLda qînlgAlûgA'n hao hao.
Here is | chief | growing himself up so great as lie sits.
DAñ kî'ñgat ugua', dAñ kî'ñgat ugua'.
You | are getting rich (or great) sitting there, | you | are getting rich (or great) sitting there.
DAñ sLû'lgAlwAñ gua'. DAñ+ qî'ñlgAlwAñ gua'.
You | are moving so greatly as you sit. | You | are highly moving as you sit.
DAñ kî'ñgat ugua', dAñ kî'ñgat ugua'.
You | are getting rich (or great) sitting there, | you | are getting rich (or great) sitting there.
DAñ sLû'lgAlwAñ gua'. DAñ+ qî'ñlgAlwAñ gua'.
You | are moving so greatly as you sit. | You | are highly moving as you sit.
DAñ sLû'lgAlwAñ gua'.
You are moving so greatly as you sit.

Here the chief causes himself to grow up greatly as he sits.
You are becoming great, you are becoming great.
You are moving so greatly as you sit. You are moving highly as you sit.
You are becoming great, you are becoming great.
You are moving so greatly as you sit. You are moving highly as you sit.
You are moving so greatly as you sit.

CHAPTER 32

[Hao] î'sîñ [a a] Lgua' [a] dAñ lalâ'ga+gaga [ha] xêga'nl
Again | I do not expect | your | screens | inside | there will be
îña'-us wagî+gâ'gîña'ñ gâ'lgalwan.
a noise | for it | (you) are crying | (you) are moving while sitting down.

I do not expect there will again be a noise inside your screens, for which you sit crying. [1]

---

[1] These words are intended as a gentle reproof, reminding the child that he is too high born to cry in that way.

CHAPTER 33

Hao î'sîñ a-a-a-a L'gua'-a-a-a Lûgûlî'na [1] xetgâ'- + dAñ xatga'
Again | perhaps | Upset-Canoe | in front of | your | father
ai+ dAñ gaLgâ'ndA[ga] dAñ galgâ'lao lîña'-us.
you | look around at new things | you | taken care of sitting | expect to be.
Aiyañê'-ê-ê-A ê-ê-êyañ â'-a-a aiyañê' q!o'ldjatga'+.
Be careful, |be careful, | chief-woman.

Hao î'sîñ a-a-a-a L'gua'-a-a-a giê'stA t!â'go xAndja'os gê
Again | perhaps | from where | copper | came | from | around
dAñ xatga' ai+ dAñ gaLgâ'ndA[ga] dAñ galgâ'lao
your | father | you | look around at new things you be taken care of sitting
lîña'-us.
expect to be.
Aiyañê'-ê-ê-A ê-ê-êyañ â'-a-a aiyañê' q!o'ldjatga'+.
Be careful, |be careful, | chief-woman.

Hao î'sîñ a-a-a-a L'gua'-a-a-a giê'stA li'mAn XA'ndjusgê
Again | perhaps | from where | hide of some mainland animal |came around
dAñ xatga' ai+ dAñ gaLgâ'ndA[ga] dAñ galgâ'lao
your father you look around at new things you be taken care of sitting
lîña'-us.
expect to be.
Aiyañê'-ê-ê-A ê-ê-êyañ â'-a-a aiyañê' q!o'ldjatga'+.

---

[1] A place north of Cape Ball.

Be careful, |be careful, | chief-woman.

Hao î'sîñ a-a-a-a L'gua'-a-a-a giê'stA gu'lxas xA'ndjus gê
Again | perhaps | from where | big variety of abalone | came around
dAñ xatga' ai+ dAñ gaLgâ'ndA[ga] dAñ galgâ'lao
your father you look around at new things you be taken care of sitting
lîña'-us.
expect to be.
Aiyañê'-ê-ê-A ê-ê-êyañ â'-a-a aiyañê' q!o'ldjatga'+.
Be careful, |be careful, | chief-woman.

Again perhaps you expect to sit up high in your father's canoe, [1] chief-woman, and look around upon all things in front of Upset-Canoe.
Be careful, be careful, chief-woman!

Again perhaps you expect to sit up high in your father's canoe, chief-woman, and look around the place whence coppers come.
Be careful, be careful, chief-woman!

Again perhaps you expect to sit up high in your father's canoe, chief-woman, and look around the place whence li'mAn-hides come.
Be careful, be careful, chief-woman!

Again perhaps you expect to sit up high in your father's canoe, chief-woman, and look around the place whence abalones come.
Be careful, be careful, chief-woman.

---

[1] Chiefs' children used to be placed high up on blankets in the centre of trading-canoes so that they could look about. Here the baby is reminded of what she used to do in a former existence.

CHAPTER 34

Agua' q!oldjat xatgâ'l++Añ Ldjîñ xâ'-idAga-i gAn
It may be chief-woman's fathers Bella Bella people with
LûsqA'sL îndjâ'wAs gu tc!aanû' djî'îña lâ'na la'-a-a-a
return by canoe | from being angry | there | the fire | next to | that one |let
agA'ñ ha-i tc!îtgâ'go gû'anda.
let watch | and tend you | while you lie about.
Gû'sta gî dâ'gâgîña'ñ galgû'lwañ?
What | for | are you crying | and sitting around as a noble sits?
Gû'sta gî dâ'gâgîña'ñ galgû'lwañ?
What | for | are you crying | and sitting around as a noble sits?

Agua' q!oldjat xatgâ'l++Añ Gwai'got xâ'-idAga-i gAn
It may be | chief-woman's | fathers Ninstints | people | with
LûsqA'sL îndjâ'wAs gu Lgia'gustA lâ'na la'-a-a-a agA'ñ
return by canoe | from being angry | there (one) next the door | to that one | let | let
ha-i tc!îtgâ'go gû'anda
watch and tend you while you lie about.
Gû'sta gî dâ'gâgîña'ñ galgû'lwañ?
What | for | are you crying | and sitting around as a noble sits?
Gû'sta gî dâ'gâgîña'ñ galgû'lwañ?
What | for | are you crying | and sitting around as a noble sits?

Perhaps when the chief-woman's fathers return from being angry with the Bella Bella people, that one (captured slave) next the fire will take care of you while you are lying about.
For what do you cry as you sit like a noble's child?

Perhaps when the chief-woman's fathers return from being angry with the Ninstints people, that one next to the door will take care of you while you are lying about.

For what do you cry as you sit like a noble's child?

CHAPTER 35

Lû'gua nAñ na'nga sL!a-i dja'kia qîndjâ'waxañ: wagi
At that time | someone's | grandmother | hand | wooden tray with square sides | has been hurt, I hear: | for it
gagîña'ñ, wagi gâ'lgalwa'ñ q!oldjida, q!oldjida, gadja'o
(you) cry, | for it | (you) sit and move around (i. e., the body), | chief-woman | chief-woman, | sit and move [1]

Perhaps you are crying and are moving around for your grandmother's hand, which was hurt on a wooden tray, chief-woman, chief-woman.

---

[1] A woman of this family had such a large hand, that she could pick up enough berries to fill a wooden tray. This story is referred to, but the wording is rather obscure.

CHAPTER 36

Dâ'gua gâ'gwaiya' gâ'gwaiya', dâ'gua, gâ'gwaiya'
You ? | (whence) have been falling | have been falling, | you ? | (whence) have been falling,
gâ'gwaiya'.
have been falling.
Dâ'gua gâ'gwaiya' gâ'gwaiya'
You ? | have been falling | have been falling
Sq!aos qâs gûs'tA gua da gâ'gwaiya' gâ'gwaiya' da
Salmon-berry bushes | top of | from | ? | you | have been falling | have been you falling
gâ'gwaiya' gâ'gwaiya'.
have been falling | have been falling.

Whence have you fallen, have you fallen? Whence have you fallen, have you fallen? [1]
Did you fall, fall, fall, fall, from the top of the salmon berry bushes?

---

[1] That is, "How did you come to us?"

CHAPTER 37

Ha-ilä' gîdona'; [1] ha-ilä' gîdona'.
Stop crying, | chief's child; | stop crying, | chief's child.
Hao îsî'ñ hî'ñ Lgua â gîtsîs gaodjuwa'-i hao dAñ gan
Again | I do not expect | chief's child's | drums | you | for
xêgîldia' lîna'gûs. Ha-i wA'gî(ñ) gagîña'ñ galgâ'lwañ.
sound | are going to. | Now | for it | crying | moving about seated.
Ha-ila' gîthû'na gadjû'gAn.
Stop crying, | great chief's child | child of noble family sits
Hai hai gîthû'na' gadjû'gAn.
Now, | now, | great chief's child | child of noble family sits.

Ha-ilä' gîdona'; ha-ilä' gîdona'.
Stop crying, | chief's child; | stop crying, | chief's child.
Hao îsî'ñ hî'ñ Lgua â gîtsîs gua'gAna'-i hao dAn gAn
Again | I do not expect | chief's child's | heavy planks | you | for
qî'ñgao dîa'o lîna'gûs. Ha-i wA'gî[ñ] gagîña'n
are going | to lay | are going to. | Now | for it | crying
galgâ'lwañ moving about seated.
Ha-ila' gîthû'na gadjû'gAn.
Stop crying, | great chief's child | child of noble family sits
Hai hai gîthû'na' gadjû'gAn.
Now, | now, | great chief's child | child of noble family sits.

Stop crying, child! Stop crying child!

---

[1] Ha-ilä' gîdona' is equivalent to Lâ'na gut u'lda nAñgida's.

I do not expect that drums will sound for you, the chief's child, again, for which you are moving about crying.
Stop crying, great chief's child!
Stop crying, great chief's child!

Stop crying, child! Stop crying, child!
I do not expect that they are going to lay heavy planks for you, the chief's child, again, for which you are moving about crying.
Stop crying, great chief's child!
Stop crying, great chief's child! [1]

---

[1] All this refers to polatching and house-building.

CHAPTER 38

Ha dîdaxui'+gî'+ anA'ñ xAñgô' lAndjî'+wa'+s la+.
Towards the woods | some one | facing | sitting down (like common people) |he (who was sitting).
Dja Lana' q!o'guga+ô+.
Say, | stop | telling lies.
DAñ siwulAndjû'gâ'+sga+[ha] djigA'ldAxwañ gî+djhao.
Your | mouth will be crooked | mosquito (i. e., common people) | people.

One sits here like a common person facing the woods.
Say, stop telling lies!
Your mouth will become crooked, mosquito people. [1]

---

[1] Some one uses the low-class word for "sitting down" to the child, and is told to stop or the wealthy will give away so many blankets as to put him to shame and "give him a bad name." That is what is meant by "your mouth will become crooked." Common people are called "mosquito people."

CHAPTER 39

HalA' sqada'l gô'ñga û skîtgadjû'giagAñ-uldies.
Come, | chief's child's | father, | sing a song for the child (accompanied by drumming) | this morning.
La agA'ña gutda'wonâ'ga hadigwa'ñ Q!ô'na qê'gawa'-i.
You | yourselves | make ready in mind | and time | Those-born-at-Skedans.

HalA' sqada'l gô'ñga û skîtgadjû'giagAñ-uldies.
Come, | chief's child's | father, | sing a song for the child (accompanied by drumming) | this morning.
La agA'ña gutda'wonâ'ga hadigwa'ñ Djî'gua al lâ'nas.
You | yourselves | make ready in mind | and time | Town-of-Djî'gua-People.

HalA' sqada'l gô'ñga û skîtgadjû'giagAñ-uldies.
Come, | chief's child's | father, | sing a song for the child (accompanied by drumming) | this morning.
La agA'ña gutda'wonâ'ga hadigwa'ñ Dâ'gAñ sêl gîda'-i.
You | yourselves | make ready in mind | and time | Common - Food-Steamers.

Come, chief's child's father, sing a song for him, accompanied by drumming, this morning!
Be ready, Those-born-at-Skedans!

Come, chief's child's father, sing a song for him, accompanied by drumming, this morning!
Be ready, Town-of-Djî'gua-People!

Come, chief's child's father, sing a song for him, accompanied by drumming, this morning!
Be ready, Common-Food-Steamers! [1]

---

[1] The families are told to be on the alert for invitations to a potlatch, when the child will be tattooed, etc.

CHAPTER 40

AdAñ gô'+ñga nagâ'ga, adAñ gô'+ñga nagâ'ga, Q!ô'na
Your | father's | house in, | your | father's | house in, | Cape Q!ô'na
kun sq!ê'na-i hao[a] ga ta goñalxa'ndies.
sea-gulls | eating things are making cries.
Ga dAñ gîdagalgâ'l uga'ñ.
All these things | you | are going to move | proudly as you sit.

AdAñ gô'+ñga nagâ'ga, adAñ gô'+ñga nagâ'ga, Gîlû'sAms
Your | father's | house in, | your | father's | house in, | Nass Inlet
kun sq!ê'na-i hao[a] ga tâ goñalxa'ndies.
sea-gulls | eating things are making cries.
Ga dAñ gîdagalgâ'l uga'ñ.
All these things | you | are going to move | proudly as you sit.

In your father's house, in your father's house, Cape Q!ô'na sea-gulls [1] make cries as they eat.
You are going to bear yourself proudly in the midst of these things.

In your father's house, in your father's house, Nass Inlet sea-gulls make cries as they eat.
You are going to bear yourself proudly in the midst of these things.

---

[1] That is, those invited to the potlatch.

CHAPTER 41

HalA' gagî'ñ gu, halA' gagî'ñ gu,
Come, | let us take (the baby) on our knees | there; come, | let us take (the baby) on our knees | there.
Gô'ñga na'ga qAli gutgî gagaga'ñ, gutgî gagaga'ñ.
Its father's | house | inside | to each other | hand it, | to each other | hand it.
HalA' gagî'ñ gu, halA' gagî'ñ gu,
Come, | let us take it on our knees, | come, | let us take it on our knees.

Come, let us take (the baby) on our knees! Come, let us take (the baby) on our knees!
Hand it to one another inside of its father's house, hand it to one another!
Come, let us take it on our knees! Come, let us take it on our knees!

CHAPTER 42

Hao da'lAñ La'a hao da'lAñ La tcîna'-i lanâ'ga [1] gut gîda
You | you | grand-father's | town | upon | chiefs' children
gAnlgaldiâ'n,
walking about,

DalA'n sgun ya'dañs gî'tsîs, dalA'ñ ya'daga.
You (are the) | only (ones) | fit to be | chiefs' children, | you | are fit to be.
Sqada'ls dalA'ñ ya'daga,
Great ones | you | are fit to be,
Gîtsî's dalA'ñ ya'daga.
Chiefs' children | you | are fit to be.

You walk about as chiefs' children in your grandfather's town.
Only you are fit to be chiefs' children.
You are fit to be sqada'l (close relatives of chiefs).
You are fit to be chiefs' children.

---

[1] Sometimes qaqa'nga ("his town"), perhaps qaga'oga, was substituted for lanâ'ga.

CHAPTER 43

Wa'Lu dî'nAñ gîda' kûxiâ'ñgwansî' Lu gîñxAn sî'lget a'ñga
At that time | my child | youth | goes around as a | when | for nothing | alone | my own
la q!â'-ugwañ.
I sit -around.

When my child becomes a youth, I shall vainly sit around alone (for he will go to live with his uncle).

CHAPTER 44

Gî'tîn-dja'tgañ îanã+ñ sû'wañ.
Eagle | woman of his own | he married | he says.
Adî'dAxua xA'nhao waga gâ'djiwañ sû'ugAñ.
Here behind us | yet | his (wife) | is sitting, | he says.
Adî'dAxua xA'nhao waga gâ'djiwañ sû'ugAñ.
Here behind us | yet | his (wife) | is sitting, | he say.
Ha'lA waga da'osgian dî'gô.
Come, | his(wife) | let us all go | and get!

Ha'lA waga da'osgian dî'gô.
Come, | his(wife) | let us all go | and get!
Adî'dAxua xA'nhao waga gâ'djiwan sû'ugAñ.
Here behind us | yet | his (wife) | is sitting, | he say.
Ha'lA waga da'osgian dî'gô.
Come, | his(wife) | let us all go | and get!

He says he has married his own Eagle woman.
Here behind us he says his wife is sitting.
Here behind us he says his wife is sitting.
Come, let us go and get her!
Come, let us go and get her!
Here behind us he says his wife is sitting.
Come, let us go and get her!

CHAPTER 45

DAñ sgu'nxA'n gua djâ'ada kudjû'diawîs,
You | are not the only one | woman | we who belong to a low family,
DAñ sgu'nxA'n gua djâ'ada kudjû'diawîs,
You | are not the only one | woman | we who belong to a low family,
Djia'djats hao qoa'nga,
Women | are plenty,
Djia'djats hao qoan kuha'oga.
Women | plenty | belonging to a low class.

You are not the only woman of our low-class family,
You are not the only woman of our low-class family.
There are plenty of women,
There are plenty of low-class women. [1]

---

[1] This contains a polite self-abasement, which is of course intended to be taken in exactly the opposite sense.

CHAPTER 46

WA'ga xê'gañ qeñgî'ndala-i (four times)
His (son or daughter) making a great noise went by on the water.
Agua ga'-idjîxuihao.
I wonder which way he is going (i. e., the child)!
WA'ga xê'gañ qeñgî'ndala-i
His (son or daughter) making a great noise went by on the water.
A'gua gwaisku'ngwi.
It must be towards the north point of the islands.

His great son (the child) went by upon the water with a great noise.
I wonder whither he is going!
His great son went by upon the water with a great noise.
Perhaps to North Island (to invite the people to a potlatch).

CHAPTER 47

Hî hîyaihîya gwa-i kî'lsLa-i hao ahai'ya aya q!ai'gîndalAñ
Island | chief | this | was coming
l gûdA'ñ hao îhî ahaiya
I thought, but
KîlsLa'-is Lua'-i L!a qêngîndala-i, hî hîyai hîya.
Chief's | canoe, | however, | comes greatly.

I thought the island chief [1] was coming,
But the chief's canoe comes greatly. [2]

---

[1] The "island chief" probably refers to Raven or another supernatural being.
[2] That is the canoe of this infant.

CHAPTER 48

Ayâ'ña kî'lsLa-i ga'ña (four times).
Be careful of | chief | my own.
Dja Lan la q!ô'gugago.
Say, | stop | biting.
DAñ si-û' djigu'ldAxwañ gîda'-i.
Your month might become crooked | mosquitoes | common things.

Be careful of my chief.
Stop biting!
Your mouth might become crooked, common mosquitoes. [1]

---

[1] The singer is probably drawing an analogy between the biting of mosquitoes and bad words used towards the rich by common people, who are called "mosquitoes."

CHAPTER 49

Dâ gut gua gagwai'ya gagwai'ya; qa'-idjis qâs gû'stA
You | your mind made up | ? | to fall into (the cradle) | to fall into (the cradle) | spruce | top | from
gagwai'ya sq!aos qâs gû'stA gagwai'ya.
to fall in; | salmon-berry bush | top | from | to fall in.

Did you make up your mind to fall (into the cradle), to fall in from the top of a spruce-tree, to fall in from the top of a salmon-berry bush?

CHAPTER 50

Â'dAñ gô'ñga nâ'gaga adA'ñ tcî'nga nâ'ga adA'ñ tcî'nga
Your | father's | house in, | your | grand-father's | house, your | grand-father's
nâ'ga,
house,
Gilû'sAms [1] sq!ê'na-i ga tagô'nalxandles ga dAñ qoya'
Nass Inlet | sea-gulls | make a noise while eating | in | you | dear
gâ'lgalwañ.
move about highly.

Â'dAñ gô'ñga nâ'gaga Lgai-û'kun sq!ê'na-i ga tagô'ñal-
Your | father's | house in | Skidegate Point | sea-gulls | make a noise while
xandies ga dAñ gî'dagalgAl.
eating | in, | you | get higher all the time (receiving more tattoo-marks, etc.)

In your father's house, in your (grandfather's house, in your grandfather's house,
Where Nass Inlet sea-gulls (i. e., the Nass people) make noises as they eat, you, dear, move highly.
In your father's house, where Skidegate Point sea-gulls (i. e., Skidegate people) make a noise as they eat, you get higher (i. e., become a greater chief) all the time.

---

[1] The second time this was sung, Q!ô'na kun ("Q!ô'na Point") was substituted for Gilû'sAms.

CHAPTER 51

Ayâ'ña î'ldjao yaña xî'lsîs gañâ'ñ gu'tgei dalA'ñ xî'ldjî
Be careful, | noble men | mine, | leaves | like to one another | you are going
qê'ndaldiasga.
to grow.
Ayâ'ña kî'lsLa-i gâ'ña, ayâ'ña kî'lsLa-i gâ'ña.
Be careful, | chief | mine! | Be careful, | chief | mine!

Be careful, my noble sons! you will grow to one another like leaves.
Be careful, my own chief! Be careful, my own chief!

CHAPTER 52

Â'gua t!a'gagua gagî'ñañ awâ'gua kî'lsLa-i?
Right here | for it | crying | sitting right here, | chief?
Â'gua t!a'gagua gagî'ñañ awâ'gua kî'lsLa-i?
Right here | for it | crying | sitting right here, | chief?

Â'gua ha'yat xA'nhao djâ'sasgaña dAñ gô'tga djî'ldasga
Right here | will not belong | your sisters | yours | sit up higher | make him,
kî'lsLa-i?
chief?
Lgâ'natsgâ'ña sq!ens is ga t'agAñalxañgA'ns gaña'ñ dAñ
Cousins (yours are) | sea-gulls | are (like) | some people | make them cry by stepping on | like | you
xê'tga sûsgî'ñgAs kî'lsLa-i.
in front of | say is going to be | chief.
Â'gua t!a'gagua gagî'ñañ awâ'gua kî'lsLa-i?
Right here | for it | crying | sitting right here, | chief?

Are you crying for it, chief?
Are you crying for it, chief?
Are you crying for your sisters, that you be seated up higher (on a pile of blankets)?
For your cousins, that there be people in front of you as numerous as if people made sea-gulls cry, being obliged to step on them,--
For those things are you crying here, chief?

CHAPTER 53

Dîga gâ'goaya+, Dîga gâ'goaya+, yê hê hê,
To me | you came, | to me | you came, | yê hê hê,
Dîga gâ'goaya, Dîga gâ'goaya.
To me | you came, | to me | you came,
Awa'-i L!a'hao dî'ga dîna'ñ ga gwaiya'gAn.
Mother | instead of some one else | to me | my child | to (me) | came walking.
Awa'-i L!a'hao dî'ga dîna'ñ gît gwaiya'gAn.
Mother | instead of another | to me | my child | chief's child | came walking.
Awa'-i gâ'dji wêhê, [1]
Mother | of noble family | mother,
Awa'-i gâ'dji awa'-i, (four times)
Mother | of noble family | mother,

You came to me, you came to me, yê hê he!
You came to me, you came to me.
You came walking to me, calling me "mother," instead of to some one else.
To me my child, who is a chief's child, came walking, calling me "mother,"
Mother of noble family,
Mother of noble family, mother of noble family, mother of noble family, mother of noble family.

---

[1] Equivalent to awa'-i.

CHAPTER 54

Gûgu's gi la gîtgîñâ'+ñ?
What | for | he (or she) | is crying like a noble's son [gît]?
Gûgu's gi la galgalwa'ñ?
What | for | he | moves around?
Atcî'na-i nâ'ga-i gî la kungîña'ñ [1] galgalwa's ahî'gua, etc.
Grandfather | the house | for | he | is crying | moves about as he is seated.

Why does he cry as a noble cries (i.e., softly)?
Why does he move around as he sits?
He moves around and cries for grandfather's house.

---

[1] Equivalent to gî'tgîñañ.

CHAPTER 55

(Words in Tlingit)

Ya'naxê, ya'naxê; â'hao; ya'naxê, ya'naxê. [1]
Gadjî'djûs dûqal dAsgî xûku yana.
his dog
WAgakîda kAda'ostêdja.

Haida Equivalent

Xa'as xA'nhao qê'gas wa'ga A'ñga k!û'gagA'ñga:
Dogs | even | when they have pups | to them | theirs | love:
Wa'alhao A'ñga ga dî k!ûga'gAñ.
That is why | mine | I | love.

Even dogs love their offspring:
So I love mine.

---

[1] This line is repeated several times.

CHAPTER 56

Îhîyîyaha, etc.
Q!êt gâ'atgê dAñ tcî'ngañ a L! dA'lgîns Lû dAñ gê'dAñgîn
Passage | through | to you | guests | come here | when | you | used to dance
gaña'ñ dAñ gêtgâ'ñAñ dâ gûdAña'owus dâ ku'ngîñansa.
like | you | to be dancing (etc.) | you | thought | to be so | you | cry for it.
LLû ga gê'dAñgîn gaña'ñ wA'ga ge'daowus.
Olden things times | were | like | that way | it is now.
XA'ldAñ dâ'gans xA'nhao gu'lxa lâs dâ'gaxida.
Slaves even (common people) | own | even | abalone-shells | good | begin | to own.
Îhiya, etc.

Îhîyîyaha, etc.
You cry because you want to dance as you used to when guests came through the strait [1] to you.
It is not now as it was in olden times.
Even slaves (that is, members of other families besides the Yaku gî'tîna-i) are beginning to own good abalone shells.
Îhiya, etc.

---

[1] The strait is probably Skidegate Channel.

CHAPTER 57

Hî hî ha hî, etc.
Lan L!a ku'ngîñañ.
Stop, | however, | crying.
Lan L!a kû'djiû.
Stop, | how-ever, | and sit down.
Lima'n sqâ'lAña-i dA'ñga gu'tgAn kûdA'sdiga,
(Kind of skin) | stowed away | yours | lies in many | caches one after the other.
Î'sîñ qâ'li gut dâ kûxiâ'ñgwa'ñgasañ
Again | inside (of house) | you | will go round.
Lan a [1] sga'-il kîlsLa'-i l qê'gAn. [2]
Stop | your | crying, | chief | I | bore.
Hî hî ha hî, etc.

Hî hî ha hî, etc.
But stop crying!
Stop and sit down!
Your limA'n blankets lie stowed away in many storehouses.
Again you will go round inside of the house.
Stop crying, chief I bore!
Hî hî ha hî, etc.

---

[1] Equivalent to la.
[2] The word dîna'ñgAn ("my son") is sometimes substituted for l qê'gAn.

CHAPTER 58

Îhî îhî hî, etc.
Gû'gus t!a'gahas dînA'ñ kûñgîñâ'ñodigañ?
What | for | my child | sits crying,
Gu'lxas t!a'ga gwA dînA'ñ kuñgîña'ño?
Abalone-shells for my child cries?
DAñ gaña'ñ gwA dî kîlsLia'wus qâñ l qê'gAn.
You | like | ? | I | sit a chief, | my uncle | I | bore.

Îhî îhî hî, etc.
For what does my child cry?
Does my child cry for abalone-shells?
Like you I sit as a chief, uncle [1] that I bore?

---

[1] One of the parents' ancestors is reborn: therefore the child is called "uncle."

CHAPTER 59

Lî'ñgua xAldâ'ñgAñ q!ô'lget [ahîyîa]
Why is it | your slave | close by,
Hao dâ îlgîyâ'gAñAñ dâ sûkû'djiwañ?
You | want something you cannot get, | you | say?
DAñ qô'naga kûdjû'geda qâñ I qê'gAn.
You | are too foolish, | my uncle I | bore.

Why do you cry for something that you cannot get,
Sitting close by your slave? [1]
You are very foolish, uncle I bore.

---

[1] The mother calls herself the child's "slave" in jest. An "uncle" is reborn in the child.

CHAPTER 60

Îhîhîa, îhîhîa (many times).
Tâ'-idAldans dî'txa xA'nhao dî'nAñ kû'sqetgwansi Lû sq!ao-
Waves behind even my child looks around when salmon-
gâns q!ana's at dî'nAñ dî gîñqô'nañgasañ.
berries unripe with my child one will fool.
Îhîhîa, îhîhîa.

Îhîhîa, îhîhîa, etc.
When my child looks around behind the waves even, she
will fool me with unripe salmon-berries. [1]
Îhîhîa, îhîhîa.

---

[1] I could get no clew to the significance of these words, which are evidently partly metaphorical.

CHAPTER 61

I hîyaha, etc.
GustA gî'hao dî'nañ kuñgîñâ'ñgAñ?
What | for | my child | cries?
Q!ô'na kun xê'txa kuLî'ndala-igi î'sîñ gê'da kuLindâ'lgasan
Q!ô'na | Point | in front of | to pass along by canoe | again | cries for that | she will travel by canoe
q!o'lgAn djâ'ga?
my master's | wife
Îhî', etc.

I hîyaha, etc.
For what is my child crying?
Does she cry to pass along again by canoe in front of Point Q!ô'na, my master's wife? [1]
Îhî', etc.

---

[1] By saying "master's wife," the singer implies that her child will marry a higher chief than herself. "Passing along again" refers to the former existence of the child. Point Q!ô'na is near Nasto.

CHAPTER 62

Ayî'hiya, ayî'hiya (many times).
Dâ îsî'ñ gut lâ'gaasañ Lgai-û' l'nagâ'-i qâñ l qê'gAn.
You | too | will be happy there | Skidegate | town, | my uncle I | bore.
Ayî'hiya, ayî'hiya (many times).

Ayî'hiya, ayî'hiya, etc.
You will again be happy there in Skidegate town, [1] uncle I bore.
Ayî'hiya, ayî'hiya, etc.

---

[1] The Yâ'ku gîtînâ'-i are said to have lived originally in the middle of Skidegate village.

CHAPTER 63

I hî'hîa.
Gû'sgihao dâ kungiñâ'ñwañ?
What | you | are crying for?
Xâ'na-qa'li gî gua dâ ku'ñgîñañ?
Skidegate Inlet | for | ? | you | cry?
Î'sîñ sta dAñ kî'iñawasañ.
Again | from | you | will have news sent around about you.

I hî'hîa.
What are you crying for?
Do you cry for Skidegate Inlet?
Again from there you will have news spread around about you (when your husband puts up a house-pole).

CHAPTER 64

GadA'ldiañ, gadA'ldiañ (many times),
How great you are, | how great you are!
Sû'digwañ gî'dadiañ, gî'dadian (last word repeated several times)
They said | belonging to a high family, | belonging to a high family
A da'lañ siñq!a'odaga agê'gî at t!â'gwus k!î'tayû'-gadas
You | gambling-stick bag | into | with | copper | throw a great one (in exchange for services)
wa'at sgun gîdâ'diañ sûdî'gwañ. [1]
with it | only | belong to a high family, | they say.

How great you are, how great you are! etc.,
They say belonging to a high family, belonging to a high family, etc.
In exchange you throw a great copper into the gambling stick bag. They say those with this are the only ones who belong to a high family.

---

[1] This is difficult to translate. Reference is made to a chief of this family who always staked a copper when he gambled, and invariably won.

CHAPTER 65

Qâ-i dî'txa+ I qî'ñgwañ qa'odî+ kî'IsLa-i Iîñ I qê'xa
Sea-Lion (Town) | behind | I | was looking around | a while, | chief | is going to be | I | found,
kA'nxida-i+.
boy just big enough to walk.
Aiyâ'ña, aiyâ'ña, kî'IsLa-igan.
Take care, | take care, | my own chief!
Aiyâ'ña qî'ñgêtgañ.
Take care, | my own master (or chief)!

While I was looking around behind Sea-Lion Town, I found the future chief, a boy just big enough to walk.
Take care, take care, my own chief!
Take care, my own master!

CHAPTER 66

Qâ-igagî+djat î+niä'nai ga ai î'î'îangAn.
A woman of Qa-i | went out and married, | went out and married.
L! lqaxiasLaia'si gu Lû qê'da-i hao gao-ula'ñ gua kî'lsLa-
They are going to call him, | there canoe | largest (i. e., chief's) | is gone in the morning, | ? | chief
igâ'+na.
my own.

One went to Sea-Lion Town to marry.
They were going to call him, but the chief's canoe was gone in the morning, my own chief. [1]

---

[1] An incident in the family history is involved. When they set out to call the chief who was going to marry, the canoe was gone. It was customary for the chief to give a canoe when one of his family married. This is probably referred to.

CHAPTER 67

Tcî'nAñ sîlgâ' nAñ kûgwai'ya [1] skoa'gagîn gê'tgagî [2] hao.
His grand-father's | place | some one | went a long time ago | behind | was there.
Lû'ga gû'ga ga sLdA'ldañ Lûgagû'ga ga qîngiñgî'ñga;
On his canoe | planks | they put on their sides | on his canoe | thing | is great on the water;
Wa'gAn dî'nA+ñ hî'dja+la-i wa'gAn dî'nAñ kudjû'gaasañ.
For it | my child | is a boy (baby word), | for it | my child | is going to be a leader.
Yâ'ña, yâ'ña, kîlsLa'-igan. Yâ'ña, yâ'ña, kî'ñgetgan.
Be careful, | be careful, | my chief! | Be careful, | be careful, | my master!

My child is a boy because he is going to do as his grandfather did when one went to his place long ago.
After he had been there, his canoe was so deeply laden (with gifts), that they had to put the weather-boards on it (to increase its capacity);
For it my child is going to be a leader.
Be careful, be careful, my chief! Be careful, be careful, my master!

---

[1] Equivalent to qa'ga.
[2] Equivalent to gê'tgaqa.

CHAPTER 68

Gut sî'+lgadaga'ñ xA'nhao kî'ga kuqêda's at (a) lA
Each other | right | after | even | names | aristocratic | with | he (baby)
kia'gañao gûdâ'gû.
call it sitting | thought he would.
KîlsLa'-i kugwê'dalañ [1] sûwa'ñ.
Chief | while walking hither | he said.
Â'yaña kî'nget gô'ñga liñga'n.
Be careful | chief's | father | is going to be!
Dî'nAñ ayâ'ña q!o'ldjat xâ'tga lîñgA'n dîna'ñ.
My child | be careful, | chief-woman | father | is going to be my child.

He thinks he would use high-sounding names, one after the other, (to the others of his own family.) [2]
He says the chief comes walking.
Be careful of the future chief's father!
Be careful of my child, the future chief-woman's father!

---

[1] Kugwê'dalañ ("while walking hither") is a low-class word referring to the chief himself.

[2] The child is supposed to call others of his family by aristocratic names, and himself by a low one.

CHAPTER 69

Qoandî'gîni qoandî'gîni kî'lsLa-i+,
There used to be plenty, | there used to be plenty, | chief,
DAñ nâ'ga ga L!a'hao qoa'ndîgînî kî'lsLa-i+;
Your | house | in | but | there used to be plenty, | chief;
Qoandî'gîni qoandî'gîni kî'lsLa-i+,
There used to be plenty, | there used to be plenty, | chief,
Qoandî'gîni qoandî'gîni kî'lsLa-i+,
There used to be plenty, | there used to be plenty, | chief,
Lgua' nAñ L! tâ'nga hû'gAñgîn kîndâ'la wA k!ia'oga gî la
While | one | they | came to by canoe, | saying hû on canoe, | great (= chief), | waiting for it | for that
gâgîñâ'ñ-galgal.
you cry and move.
Qoandî'gîni, qoandî'gîni kî'lsLa-i; qoandî'gîni, qoandî'gîni,
There used to be plenty, | there used to be plenty, | chief, there used to be plenty, | there used to be plenty.
kî'lsLa-i.
chief.

There used to be plenty, there used to be plenty, chief,
There used to be plenty in your house, chief;
There used to be plenty, there used to be plenty, chief;
There used to be plenty, there used to be plenty, chief.

You cry and move about to see them come by canoe (to the potlatch), great chief.
There used to be plenty, there used to be plenty, chief;
there used to be plenty, there used to be plenty, chief.

CHAPTER 70

Ala qî'ñgugâ'ñgaña'-i, ala qî'ñgugâ'ñgaña'-i.
I | used to see it, | I | used to see it.
DAñ nâ'gaga la'ahao tǃaogô's gôdâ'gañas hao gut at
Your | house to | I | copper | used for making boxes | now | each with other
gatkîñdagA'ñdiesi al [1] dAñ kî'îña kî'nlgalugani.
make a noise by knocking against | with | you | news of | goes about as you move about.
Ala qî'ñgugâ'ñgaña'-i, ala qî'ñgugâ'ñgaña'-i. (an indefinite number of times).
I | used to see it, | I | used to see it.
DA'ñ nâ'gaga la'ahao malê'lga-i lga'djudia's (so) a'l dAñ
Your | house in | cranberry-bushes, | grew of | you
kî'îña kî'nlgAluganî.
news of | goes about.
Ala qî'ñgugâ'ñgaña'-i, ala qî'ñgugâ'ñgaña'-i.
I | used to see it, | I | used to see it.

I used to see it, I used to see it.
News went about that boxes made of coppers in your house sounded as they knocked one another.
I used to see it, I used to see it.
News went about of cranberry-bushes growing in your house.
I used to see it, I used to see it.

---

[1] Equivalent to at ("with").

CHAPTER 71

Û+hua', [1] û+hua', ûhua'-a-a,
Loftiest one, | loftiest one, | loftiest one,
DAñ nâ'ga ga L!a qoa'ndîgînî gua kî'lsLa-i.
Your | house | in there was formerly plenty, | ? | chief.
Gî'na uhua', uhua', qâli sku'na yûdA'lgAñAs a,
Something, | greatest one, | greatest one, | inside (some thing) big | smells strongly,
U'hua, û'hua, qî'ndal?
Loftiest one, | loftiest one, | mightiest one?

Loftiest one, loftiest one, loftiest one,
There used to be plenty in your house, chief.
Does not something big (i. e., a whale) smell strongly in your house,
Loftiest, loftiest, mightiest chief?

---

[1] Ûhua' is a very high word, only applied to one or two chiefs who attained especially great power.

CHAPTER 72

Û'hua qînda'l, û'hua qînda'l (la)
Mightiest | chief, | mightiest | chief,
T!ak!î'ngâña ga La' qî'nwa-i gaatxA'n qî'ndju,
His own children | go to (to be born) | (be born from) come out of | without it (why not) | chief,
Û'hua qînda'l, û'hua qînda'l, û'hua qînda'l, la?
Mightiest | chief, | mightiest | chief, | mightiest | chief?
Û'hua qînda'l, û'hua qînda'l la,
Mightiest | chief, | mightiest | chief,
Gî'sto dAñ Lû yû'ga a'wañ qî'ndju,
Who | you | as | large | settled down | chief,
Û'hua qînda'l, û'hua qînda'l?
Mightiest | chief, | mightiest | chief?

Mightiest chief, mightiest chief,
Why did not he (Gadaga') choose to be born from his own grandchildren (instead of from some of his sisters' children), chief,
Mightiest chief, mightiest chief, mightiest chief?
Mightiest chief, mightiest chief,
Who is settled down into such affluence as he (Gadaga'), [1]
Mightiest chief, mightiest chief?

---

[1] Gadaga', according to story, was the greatest chief of the People-of-Sea-Lion-Town.

CHAPTER 73

Î'djîsigwA'ns gî dî'nAñ gwa'wañ sû'wasi.
Not a common woman at all | my child | he refuses | says.
Wa'gî dî'+nAñ gwa'wañ nAñ sû'wasi.
To it | my child | refuses, | some one | says.
A'ñga xA'nhao înasû'wa gîtî'n-djats xAn A'ñga ina'suwê+,
His own | just there | wants that one | Eagle-woman | yet | his | says he wants that one,
A'ñga xA'nhao înasî'ñgwañ.
His own | just there | he will marry.

Even a noble woman my child says he refuses.
One says he refuses her.
He wants just that Eagle woman for himself (indicating a particular one),
Just that one he will marry.

CHAPTER 74

Dja'+djâts L!aha'o lâ, dja'+djâts L!aha'o lâ.
Women are better (than men), women are better (than men).
Dja'+djâts L!a kîñgê'diasLa.
Women have more property.

KîlsLa-i'gan k!îsLa'-i dAñ gê'tgwañ axAn?
My chiefs men of one's own family) | chiefs | you | are | where?

Women are better (than men), women are better (than men).
Women have more property.
Chiefs of my family, where are you?

CHAPTER 75

Êya hâ hiê', etc.
Qâ'gaigaña nâ'ga L!ao Skî'lsîs xê'gAndigi wa'di kuñgîña'ñ uga'-i.
Uncles | houses in | but | Skî'lsîs | makes a noise (potlatch) | for it | (he or she) is crying.
Wa'di kû'djiwa ê'ya hâ hîê!, etc.
For it | sits greatly.

Êya hâ hiê', etc.
But he (or she) is crying for the noise Skî'lsîs (now reborn) makes in his uncles' houses (at the potlatch).
For it he sits greatly.

CHAPTER 76

Gîsta L!ao daga'sado sî'liya dâ skA'ndAñ kudjû'gi[gê+]
Who | but | will own it | after it | you | are crying | are sitting
dô'nê aldjî'wai? [1]
younger brother | are sitting?

But do you sit crying over who will afterwards own it, younger brother of good family?

---
[1] Or kû'djiwai.

CHAPTER 77

Â'gua nâ'nAñ Lga gut dî'nañ ku-i-ê'ndalane.
It was | his grand-mother's | land | upon | my child | walks (a proud word).
Wa'gan st!a'ga kudja'oanê.
For it | his foot | is dear.
GAm la ku'ñgîñañ Añ.
Not | you | cry (excl.)!

My child walks proudly upon his grandmother's land.
His dear foot is for that (i. e., to walk on it).
Do not cry!

CHAPTER 78

Nanaiga'ña LAga' sgâ'nas gu'lxas q!olda's Lû sgâ'nas gî
Grandmother's | land | supernatural beings | abalone-shells | stole | when supernatural beings to
h kiä'igañgîn.
I | called.
GAm gîn gu dê gudA'ñañ hai.
Nothing | I wish to eat (?) | now.

When the supernatural beings stole abalone-shells from grandmother's land, I called to the supernatural beings. Nothing I wish to eat (?).

CHAPTER 79

Tcî'nAñ lû'ga giû'gulaga, tcî'nAñ lû'ga giû'gulaga.
Grand-father's | wave | listens for, | grand-father's | wave | listens for.
StA L!ao tcînA'ñ sî'ga gut kû'djûgiagandalanê.
After it | but | grand-father's | sea | upon | goes along stopping often on the way (upon the water).

(He) listens for grandfather's [1] wave, he listens for grandfather's wave;
But afterwards he goes along upon grandfather's sea, stopping every now and then on the way.

---

[1] The "grandfather" here referred to is probably Raven.

CHAPTER 80

Â'gua nâ'nAñ Lga gut kû'lgalguña'-i gAn wagA'n sL!a'gA
Here is | her grand-mother's | land | upon | walking about | for | for it | use (your) hands
kudjâ'wan. [1]
dear.

Use your hands, my dear, to walk about upon grandmother's land.

---

[1]Kudjâ'wan is also a "high word" for "to sit."

CHAPTER 81

Gia'gAñ L!ao yuâ'ndaga-i, gia'gAñ L!ao yuâ'ndaga-i.
My crests (or figures), | however, | are very large; | my crests, | however, | are very large.
Hao q!a'lîñAs yuâ'ndaga-i, hao q!a'lîñAs yuâ'ndaga-i.
This | image | is very large, | this | image | is very large.
Gia'gAñ L!ao yuâ'ndaga-i, hao q!a'lîñAs yuâ'ndaga-i.
My crests, | however, | are very large, this | image | is very large.
La L!ao gaogê'ldasañ, la L!ao gaogê'ldasañ.
I | them | will put away, | I | them | will put away.
Hao q!a'lAñAs yuâ'ndaga-i, hao q!a'lAñAs yuâ'ndaga-i.
This | image | is very large, | this | image | is very large.

My crests (as carved) are very large, my crests are very large.
This image is very large, this image is very large.
My crests are very large, this image is very large.
I will put them away, I will put them away.
This image is very large, this image is very large.

CHAPTER 82

A LAga-i yuku'ndjudasi î'ñgut sgâ'nas û dalA'ñ yê'dada-dîgînî.
This | land is a point (Rose Spit) | on | supernatural beings | those | you | left.

Supernatural beings used to leave you on this point of land (i. e., Rose Spit).

CHAPTER 83

HawA'nô qô'godAñ Skî'lsîs l'nagâ'-i.
Still | stands | Skî'lsîs's | town.
GAm l dî'gu ku'ñgîñañAñ.
Not | upon me (my knees) | cry.

Skî'lsîs's town still stands.
Do not cry upon my knees!

CHAPTER 84

Yên dAñ î'skudals Lû gAm l dî'gu ku'ñgîñañAñ hAñ.
Truly | you are chief (or "dear") if not you on my (imp.) (knees) cry!
Dî gwa ga lgaiqendigwA'ñus.
I | am not rich.

If you are truly a chief (reborn), do not cry upon my knees!
I am not rich. [1]

---

[1] The child is scolded as being a reborn chief, and too great to cry.

CHAPTER 85

Gû'gus t!ao dAñ sû'kudjiwañ gia'ga t!a'gwa?
What | for | you | are crying | things (clothing) | for?
WAsk!iên a'ña dAñ giA'nda kudjû'asañ.
But | yours | you | shall wear | chief (or "dear").

For what do you cry, chief (or dear)? For clothing?
You shall wear it, chief (or dear).

CHAPTER 86

Nañ gêst' dî'na qoga'-iwas Lû naas gadô' dî'na kû'sqedA-
Out of his house | mine | goes out | when, | house | around | mine | will | walk
gwañasañ.
and look.
Î'ldjao dA'ñAl kuda'ltc!aasañ.
Chief (or rich man)| with | my dear will enter.

When my child goes out of his house, he will walk around among the houses and look about.
With chiefs (only) my dear will enter.

CHAPTER 87 [1]

DAñ tcîn lk!iä'nao dAn dA qä'tcû kû'udAñ.
Your | grand-father | by stick (cedar trunk used for canoe) | you | for | is looking | chief's son (or "dear").
GA'il?Añ kû'sLîgAl.
To yourself | go straight up.

Your grandfather's canoe is looking for you, dear.
Go straight up to it.

---

[1] Sung also as a "proud song" (?â'l?agadAñ s?â'lAna-i).

CHAPTER 88

ULa'mAn gî'lgîgasLas Lû tc!a'Añ gut ku'sgetgîñ.
ULa'mAn | is on the sea (in sight) | when his canoe companions | upon | the captain looked about.
A l agA'ñ kî'lSLia kudjû'da.
Make yourself a chief's son, | dear.
Haiya kî'lsLa-i, haiya kî'lsLa-i, ha'oîsîn kî'lsLa-igan.
Now | chief, | now | chief, | again | chief.

When ULa'mAn [1] lay in sight on the sea, the captain looked about upon his companions (allowing them to relax their efforts).
Make yourself a chief's son, dear.
Again he is a chief, is a chief, is a chief.

---

[1] ULa'mAn is a long, low hill near Rose Spit, generally the first sighted by canoes from Port Simpson and neighboring places in the Tsimshian country. The mother is probably thinking of the time when her child will come home from trading with the Tsimshian. A third song, which I was unable to obtain in Haida, tells in the first verse about intermarriages between the young men of the Skî'daoqao and young women of the StA'stas; in the second verse, of intermarriage with women of the Gîtî'ns of Masset.

MOURNING SONGS

CHAPTER 89

Hao gua dAñ qâ'gulAgî.
? | you | are going down.
Djîgô'es gu qagû'lAga kuda'l.
Sun there is going down, dear.

Are you going down?
The sun there is going down, dear, [1]

---

[1] The dead man is likened to the sun.

CHAPTER 90

Qeda'o gu wa qeda'o gu wa, gada'-i li qêga'na.
War men | ? | killed [1] you, |war men | ? | killed dear daughter | I | bore you
Qeda'o gwa wa, qêda'o gwa wa.
War men | ? | killed you, | war men | ? | killed you.

Did warriors kill you, did warriors kill you, dear daughter that I bore?
Did warriors kill you, did warriors kill you?

---

[1]Literally, "did."

CHAPTER 91

Qoangê'dAñ, qoangê'dAñ, qoya'sga
It becomes too much, | it becomes too much, | dear.
Qoangê'dAñ, qoangê'dAñ, qoya'sga
It becomes too much, | it becomes too much, | dear.
Qoangê'dAñ, qoangê'dAñ, qoya'sga
It becomes too much, | it becomes too much, | dear.
Qoangê'dAñ, qoangê'dAñ, qoya'sga
It becomes too much, | it becomes too much, | dear.

It becomes too much, it becomes too much, dear. [1]
It becomes too much, it becomes too much, dear.
It becomes too much, it becomes too much, dear.
It becomes too much, it becomes too much, dear.

---

[1]That is, my grief is too great to bear.

CHAPTER 92

Gû'stas Lî'nañ a q!ê'nañ ana'ñ xî'ladîgwañdañ?
What | (nothing) | myself | certain thing | shall use for medicine?
Gû'stas Lî'nañ a q!ê'nañ ana'ñ xî'ladîgwañdañ?
What | (nothing) | myself | certain thing | shall use for medicine?
Q!ê'nañ a dî Alkû'skîdêgwañ.
For myself | I | have nothing.
Qoya's dAñ xAñhîña'-i.
Dear | your | face.

What medicine shall I use (in my affliction)?
What medicine shall I use?
I have nothing to comfort me.
Your dear face (I long for).

CHAPTER 93 [1]

Qo-ês LLî'ñalAñ ?a-i l kusî't!Al.
Clouds | open with your hands | through, | look down.
DAñ lû'yîña-i dAñ xA'ñîña-i.
Your | body all | your | face all (we wish to see).

Parting the clouds with your hands, look down (from Tâ'xet's house).
We wish to see your body and your face.

---

[1] Sung only by the women of this family.

CHAPTER 94 [1]

K!iwa'-i L! nAñ qä'ñAs Lû gwî nAñ qa'-idañ.
The trail (of the dead) | but | one | could see | if | upon | one (= I) | could go,
Gwai'yê dAñ â'ldjiwa-i.
Elder brother, | your | whole body.

If I could see the trail (of the dead), I would enter upon it.
Elder brother, (I want to see) your whole body.

---

[1] Sung by a man named Skîlqoê'Las for his brother.

CHAPTER 95 [1]

Gîn st!ê'dîguña-i gwai'yai,
Something (= you) makes my heart sick (or very sad), | elder brother,
Gîn st!ê'dîguña-i.
Something makes my heart sick.

Something (i. e., the loss of you) makes my heart sick, elder brother.
Something makes my heart sick.

---

[1] Sung by the same man as Song 94.

CHAPTER 96

Ha'k!un dAñ gudA'ns k!iên gu gAm qe'id LAk!ala ?a dî
Like that | you | thought | although | ? | not | tree | shelter of | in
dAñ q!a'odañ-ûdja.
you | seated me?

If you thought so (i. e., if you chose to die), why did you not seat me in the shelter of a tree? [1]

---

[1] The last part of this is metaphorical. It means, "Why did you die so suddenly?"

CHAPTER 97

[This was composed by Qadjiqô'ku when his niece was drowned in Q!a'nAn River, and her body could not be found.]

Gû'stas, gî l da'-indAgwAñgAñ?
What | for | I | poor one | searching?
Hâ'djadia nâ'da-i.
Alas! | my niece.

For what am I, unfortunate one, looking?
Alas! my niece.

CHAPTER 98 [1]

LA'gas dAñ qä'ñ kû'gits Lû agA'ñ l kû stAñ gî'ndagiâ'ñaxAñ.
Land | you | see, | beloved one | when | yourself, | dear (or chief), | two | if you made in canoe.

If you had seen land, beloved, you would have saved yourself, dear. [2]

---

[1] Sung by the wife of one lost at sea.
[2] This is merely the sense of the Haida.

CHAPTER 99

GAm la î'L!dA qe'gaxañgo (repeated over and over).
Not | you at us | look.

Do not look at us.

CHAPTER 100 [1]

DalA'ñ gu kî'lsta-us dî L!ao gAm kî'lstastA dî gudA'ñhAñgAn.
Your | ? | voices are tired, | I | but | not | have a tired voice | I | want to.

Your voices are tired, but I do not want to have a tired voice (i. e., I do not want to cease wailing).

---

[1] Perhaps a song of the LîêlAñ qê'awa-i.

MISCELLANEOUS SONGS

CHAPTER 101

Â'gua Skî'lsîs I'nagâ'-i ʔai'ya gagô'das hô.
Here | Skî'lsîs's | town | lies.
DAñ gua gû'la dô'na-i (repeated four times).
You | ? | think it good | younger brother?

Here lies Skî'lsîs's town.
Are you pleased with it, younger brother? [1]

---

[1] The "younger brother" is perhaps a captive or an opponent in battle.

CHAPTER 102 [1]

[Sung around the head of an enemy raised upon a pole.]

You Tsimshian people are foolish. Are you like coppers? [2]

---

[1] I was able to obtain only the translation of this song.
[2] Because they were fearless in battle.

CHAPTER 103

[Song by women during the absence of their husbands with a war-party.]

Sk!A'ga-o t!a'êt qô'nagAñ.
Sk!A'ga, | this one | killed | many people.

Sk!A'gao killed (and enslaved) many people.

CHAPTER 104

Yêl dî tâda's Lû q!e'nañ dî u'nsAtsgaiya'ndô.
Raven | me | ate | if | myself | I | would not know.
Ao Lîsînôt dAga'ñ I sû'g.
Now | first time | for myself | I | am singing.

If Raven had eaten me, [1] I would not know myself.
Now for the first time I am singing to myself.

---

[1] "Being eaten by Raven" seems to mean being killed in war.

CHAPTER 105

Xâ'La gwai'yê gô'lgal q!ê'aosgiên.
Haidas' | island | green | has become.

The island of the Haida has become green (i. e. the hats have appeared as when spring comes and the foliage turns green.)

CHAPTER 106

Laugh at the chief! for, although he is a chief, he has no rattle in his hand.

www.ingramcontent.com/pod-product-compliance
Lightning Source LLC
Chambersburg PA
CBHW040108100526
44584CB00029BA/3930